Deb Nawrotzki

MW00582644

FREEDOM TO FAIL

How do I foster risk-taking and innovation in my classroom?

Andrew K.
MILLER

ASCD Alexandria, VA USA

Website: www.ascd.org
E-mail: books@ascd.org

www.ascdarias.org

Printed in the United States of America. Cover art © 2015 by ASCD. ASCD publications present a variety of viewpoints. The views expressed or implied in this book should not be interpreted as official positions of the Association.

PAPERBACK ISBN: 978-1-4166-2038-9   ASCD product # SF115044

Also available as an e-book (see Books in Print for the ISBNs).

Library of Congress Cataloging-in-Publication Data

Miller, Andrew K.
  Freedom to fail : how do I foster risk taking and innovation in my classroom? / Andrew K. Miller.
     pages cm
  Includes bibliographical references and index.
  ISBN 978-1-4166-2038-9 (pbk. : alk. paper) 1. Educational innovations. 2. Creative teaching. 3. Classroom environment. 4. Failure (Psychology) 5. Risk-taking (Psychology) I. Title.
  LB1027.M466 2015
  371.102—dc23   2015016593

23 22 21 20 19 18 17 16 15   1 2 3 4 5 6 7 8 9 10

FREEDOM TO FAIL

How do I foster risk-taking and innovation in my classroom?

Want to earn a free ASCD Arias e-book?
Your opinion counts! Please take 2–3 minutes to give
us your feedback on this publication. All survey
respondents will be entered into a drawing to
win an ASCD Arias e-book.

Please visit

www.ascd.org/ariasfeedback

Thank you!

Redefining Failure

Failure, for most of us, is a negative concept. Students who fail to do their work do poorly in school, and workers who fail to do their jobs get fired. But failure can be positive, too: in the worlds of technology and design, for example, taking risks that generate failure is considered necessary for innovation. If failure is the end of the road in some instances, it can be the beginning of an innovative journey in others.

Unfortunately, schools tend to treat failure as almost exclusively negative. Think back to a time when you failed a test or a quiz or failed to complete an assignment. Do you remember that sinking feeling that there was nothing more you could do? I remember preparing for a big history exam in middle school. There hadn't been any quizzes leading up to the exam, so I didn't know what to expect—short-answer questions? An essay question? Multiple-choice questions? Because I was unprepared for the format of the exam, I got a mediocre score, and I wasn't given an opportunity to retake the test. My failure, in this case, was treated as exclusively negative and *final*. But when treated as a necessary step toward innovation, failure can help students to

- Promote and establish a growth mindset,
- Build resiliency and a life-long learning mentality, and
- Prepare for the real world.

So, what are we waiting for? Isn't it time we encouraged students to embrace failure as fun, exciting, and filled with possibility rather than as something to dread?

Changing Mindsets   *Fail Forward*

Fear of failure is one of the leading causes of anxiety for students. We've all been fearful of screwing up a presentation or getting an *F* on a test. But if we frame failure through a growth mindset, we can mitigate students' fears of it and even have them embrace the idea that they can "fail forward." What if we recast the word *fail* as an acronym that stands for "First Attempt in Learning"? By talking about failure in this way, we reinforce the idea that failure is a beginning rather than an end. And our actions should match our words: We should do what we can to encourage students to grow from failure.

First attempt in learning

According to Judy Willis, a leading expert on the brain and learning, "fear of risking mistakes reduces the active participation and construction of knowledge because the sensory input (instruction) cannot pass through the RAS (reticular activating system) and amygdala to the prefrontal cortex" (Willis, 2014). When we fear failure, the chemistry of the brain literally gets in the way of more learning. Indeed, research has shown that people who don't have a growth mindset are much less likely to seek out constructive feedback on their work or to be interested in further learning than those who do (Dweck, 2006).

We all want to protect children from failure, but we are actually doing them a disservice if we protect them too much. If students are never given the opportunity to fail, they'll never know how much they can improve. Students who are unaccustomed to failure may become impatient with challenging schoolwork and devalue anything that they don't get correct on the first try (Dweck, 2006).

Resiliency and Life-Long Learning

One reason to prepare students for failure is that it is inevitable; as Thomas Hoerr says, "failure is something we will all face and fostering grit prepares us for it" (2013, p. 40). By allowing and even promoting productive failure in the classroom, we can help students build their resiliency. After all, failure is an indication of what still needs to be learned. Resiliency and perseverance, which are honed through failure, are key life-long skills for students.

When we fail in safe ways, we want to learn more. Our frustration in the face of failure can help us to develop the grit we need to succeed. Consider sports teams: They may lose game after game, but they always get right back to practicing—that is, to learning new strategies, plays, and skills to improve their success rate. If a team never failed, it would never be motivated to improve.

Real-World Learning

Rote learning is a thing of the past. We now know that students learn best through authentic experiences connected to the real world (Miller, 2014). It is important, therefore, to communicate the real-world relevance of basic skills to students. We must know how to write properly so that we can one day communicate effectively at work; we must learn math skills to keep our checkbooks balanced; we must learn about color and light if we wish to appreciate great works of art. When we connect learning to authentic experiences, students see that it is necessary first to fail if they want one day to succeed in the real world.

To adequately prepare for their collegiate and professional careers students need to develop their executive-functioning skills, especially reasoning, judgment, critical analysis, and cognitive flexibility (Willis, 2014). Developing cognitive flexibility is particularly important when it comes to positive failure, as it enables us to consider multiple points of view and to approach challenges in different ways. As Willis (2014) notes, we need to "provide experiences to build flexibility to change and increase future comfort adapting to the inevitable changes that will part of [students'] lives." Our students will always experiences failures, and only more so as they grow into adulthood. When we leverage failure effectively in the classroom, we are cultivating cognitive flexibility in students.

Components of Positive Failure

All students deserve an opportunity to fail, to learn from their failure, and to move forward in their learning journey. Ensuring that they face these experiences requires intentional planning both of instructional procedures and of classroom culture. Many moving parts must be in place for failure to be an effective learning tool.

Classroom Culture

If we want students to truly value and learn from failure, we must be intentional about creating a culture that gives them the freedom to do so. By establishing classroom norms and routines that support a safe environment, we can provide students with the scaffolding they need as they fail forward. It is imperative that students have a hand in developing classroom norms so that they feel invested in making them work. Many teachers even have students create norms for classroom teams and groups, ensuring that these, too, are safe spaces for failure. When drafting norms, teachers and students should include statements about how they plan to approach failure.

Relationships and Trust

If students are going to be asked to take risks, feel safe, and learn from their failures, then they absolutely must trust their teachers, so it is imperative that we build strong relationships with them. Yes, it takes time, but it's an investment well made: The more we show students that we're interested in them as individuals and want them all to succeed, the more willing they are to participate—and, importantly, to take risks without worrying about failure. Strategies teachers can use to learn more about their students include learning style inventories, student surveys, and one-on-one interviews at the beginning of the year. Teachers can also commit to greeting every student personally as he or she enters their class and to thank them individually as they leave.

Consider taking the time to discuss students' nonacademic interests with them, as this can provide you with a strong bonding experience. Many of our students think we are a lot less like them than we really are—a myth we must work to dispel. As you work to build relationships, ask yourself: How do your students feel welcome in your class? What obstacles are getting in the way of making students feel welcome? What can I do to make students feel more welcome and safe in my classroom?

A Culture of Inquiry *generate own questions*

Establishing a culture of inquiry is critical if students are to embrace failure as a learning opportunity. To that end, teachers should construct (or co-construct with students) questions that prompt further student questioning (Wiggins & McTighe, 2013). For example, consider a group of students engaged in designing a bridge for class. The teacher might ask them, "How do we design a bridge that will hold the most weight?" This question is designed to turn power over to the students so they can generate their own questions. It's a good idea to post questions such as these prominently in the classroom. In fact, the walls of the room should honor questions and inquiry rather than answers. As students fail forward in their learning, knowing that they will have the opportunity to ask further questions helps them feel safe. The important thing isn't getting the bridge design right the first time, but rather asking questions and taking risks. And when questions have more than one right answer, students are more likely take risks.

It is sometimes a challenge for teachers serving as facilitators of inquiry to listen carefully and patiently to students. When teachers listen carefully, they can ask the right probing and clarifying questions to push students toward deeper inquiry. By asking questions, teachers are also modeling a culture of inquiry and presenting themselves as fellow inquirers rather than purveyors of all knowledge.

Discussions about Failure

When teachers set norms for the classroom at the beginning of the year, they should also share norms related to failure with students. Socratic seminars can be effective vehicles for discussing the different aspects of failure. These discussions can be paired with selections of powerful quotes, inspiring news stories, and selections from biographies. Here are some questions to consider when setting norms about failure with students:

- Why do we fail?
- Why is a failure a valuable opportunity?
- How can we fail in a productive way?
- What can we learn from this person about failure?

Taking the time to discuss failure with students helps to create a culture where the concept is not always considered a negative. In essence, teachers are imparting a new vocabulary to students that allows them to construct their own knowledge about failure and make powerful discoveries about it.

Celebrating Mistakes as Well as Successes

One of the most powerful things teachers can do to promote the freedom to fail is to acknowledge failures as they happen. When we do this, we encourage students to persevere. Teachers should also acknowledge their own mistakes when they make them: We've all had those days when we know that we could have done better by our students. When that happens, teachers can build trust with students and model embracing failure as a learning opportunity. When students see us admitting our mistakes, they see that everyone makes them and learns from them.

High-Quality Work and High Expectations

One of the critical pillars for the freedom to fail is high expectation for all students. We must believe that all students can reach their full potential. If we shoot for the middle ground, then we will get just that. As students fail, we must begin with the end in mind; we must know what the high-quality work with look like. More importantly, we must make our expectations transparent to students. If students do not believe that they can make progress towards their learning goals, then they will not embrace failures as learning opportunities but rather feel defeated. If, however, we believe in students, we can coach them through their failures to reach their full potential.

It's really easy to settle for less as students fail, especially if they fail a lot. Multiple failures can be fatiguing for both the teacher and student. If we don't encourage students to persevere regardless, we communicate to them that we expect less of them than we do of their peers. Word can get around the classroom, and an inconsistent message can undermine the freedom to fail. Some students may take 3 tries on an assignment, others might take 10—they are all different, and we must expect high-quality work from all.

Walls that Honor Failure

It is a good idea to post quotes that reframe or speak to the power of failure on walls around the classroom. Walls can talk, and as student eyes wander, as they often do, they may come across quotes that will inspire them to fail forward. Images of prominent figures who have failed can also help students reconsider the negativity of failure. It's worth changing out these quotes on a regular basis or considering digital walls that can do this automatically. If you are a blended or fully online teacher, prominently place inspirational quotes on your learning management system or inside digital module pages.

Another idea is to create create pithy phrases out of failure-related acronyms. Here are some examples:

Failure is an OPTION:

- Ongoing: Failure can happen multiple times.
- Practice: Failure is only one step in the learning process.
- Tinkering: Failure involves experimentation.
- Intentional: Failure should be productive.
- Okay: Failure is normal.
- Necessary: Failure provides rich learning.

FAIL stands for

- First
- Attempt
- In
- Learning

Teachers often post examples of outstanding student work in the classroom to show what they expect from students. I would suggest going further and posting examples of work at all stages of the journey, from the first step to the final result. Teachers should consider selecting student work that tells a story of failing forward. Appending the students' own reflections about failure can provide a powerful visual narrative of the learning process.

Room Set Up to Encourage Failing Forward

When students are seated in rows, the arrangement communicates a message of rigidness and lack of collaboration, which works against a culture of failing forward. A more flexible arrangement communicates that a more open approach to learning. If the desks in your room aren't easily moveable, try creating pods, triads, or other structures that communicate collaboration.

In addition to flexible seating arrangements, classrooms should include spaces where students are invited to experiment. Makerspaces, circles, and unassigned tables communicate the idea of learning as an open and experimental process. Another good idea is for teachers to position their desks in non-traditional spots, such as in the middle of the classroom, to encourage a different perspective. Secondary teachers would do well to borrow from elementary teachers' inclinations for workshop and learning stations, as they communicate the playful and flexible side of learning. Experiment with the overall setup of the classroom to communicate tinkering, experimentation, collaboration, flexibility, and problem solving.

Here are some other ideas for communicating openness and embracing experimentation in the classroom:

- Worktables with materials that students can use to experiment and create
- Small-group instruction tables and whole-group instruction centers
- A dedicated space for classroom presentations
- Quiet corners for reflection
- Tables of different heights for sitting and standing
- Movable whiteboards
- A mix of traditional and non-traditional seating options (bean bags, stools)
- Open spaces without furniture

Rigorous Work for Productive Failure

Because failure can happen at any time in the learning process, it is crucial that teachers anticipate possible failures and plan accordingly. If students don't feel that the work they are doing is meaningful, authentic, and/or challenging, they will likely not engage in failing forward. If we want students to persevere, then the work they do needs to matter. We should *want* our students to fail multiple times as they work, and they can only do so if we hold high expectations for them. Although it is important for students to locate, practice, and solve problems, true rigor occurs when students design problems, argue about them, and justify their conclusions (Daggett, 2014). By aiming for higher order thinking, we can ensure productive failure along the way.

A task's degree of rigor needs to be appropriate both to students' grade levels and individual abilities. If the challenge is too hard, failure may simply feel like a confirmation that the task is too much to handle—and if it's too easy, they won't experience failure at all. A good rule of thumb is to design units that are just slightly above students' ability levels (Van der Veer, 2007).

Clear Expectations and Objectives

Failure can only move students in the right direction if they have clear expectations and objectives, which are best established through rubrics and checklists and should be based on learning outcomes or standards. To encourage student buy-in, teachers might want to draft the criteria for the "Meets" section of the rubric and allow students to contribute to the "Exceeds" or "Approaches" sections. Rubrics must be written in clear language that students can understand—they shouldn't "sound like a teacher." Checklists are also a great way to make minimum expectations transparent and clear to students. Expectations must articulate a roadmap for the process of failing forward.

Authentic Challenges and Scenarios

Failure needs to be framed within the context of real-world thinking and learning. To that end, students should take on roles that mirror those they will one day take after leaving school—roles as architects, reporters, engineers, graphic designers, and the like. Here are some examples:

- Students take on the role of engineers to produce a scientifically sound airplane wing *as a means of refining* their physics and math skills.
- Students take on the role of poets to write verse about the homeless youth in their community *as a means of refining* their literary skills.
- Students take on the role of zookeepers to design zoo exhibits that meet the needs of different animals *as a means of refining* their learning of wildlife and the ecology.
- Students take on the role of doctors to diagnose hypothetical patients *as a means of refining* their learning of the human anatomy.

You'll notice some patterns in the above examples. When we *refine* our skills, we accept that we'll make mistakes along the way. Through authentic scenarios and challenges, students will experience failure in meaningful ways as they refine their learning.

Authentic Products and Work

Can we take a break from the traditional essay, please? Engaging students in failing forward not only requires them to take on real world roles, but also to design and create products that have relevance in the real world. Instead of an essay, have students write proposals, letters, pamphlets, news reports, podcast, websites, and so on.

Mrs. Cruz has always used the bridge-design challenge as a STEM activity in her classroom. It's fun and engaging for some students, but others don't seem to care about it much. Reflecting on her students' lack of enthusiasm, Mrs. Cruz decides to refine the lesson for greater real-world relevance. She and her students live in Washington State, which is famous for its poorly designed bridges, so she decides to have her students act as architects and design or retrofit bridges for greater safety. For added real-world context, Mrs. Cruz asks her students to present their findings to actual architects for feedback. The students create blueprints and proposals for building the bridges.

When students know that they'll be sharing their authentic products with an authentic audience, they will be motivated to continually revise their work as they make mistakes. Authenticity can create the need to improve work and, in the process, embrace the virtues of failure.

Authentic Assessments by Real World Experts and Guests

Authentic assessment of authentic work is essential. We often bring parents and other community members into our classrooms to provide students with feedback and praise, which ups the stakes for students. Outside visitors can demonstrate to students that even the most successful people make and learn from mistakes. Throughout the year, teachers should ask experts in a variety of fields to visit their classrooms and discuss how they learned from failing in their careers. When students see that even adults and experts in high-stakes jobs experience failure, they are more likely to feel comfortable taking risks.

Small and Intentional Failures

Students who only experience catastrophic failure will never view failure as a positive. For example, when we ask students to write an essay but only give them a single chance to revise a rough draft before affording the final grade, we aren't giving the students enough leeway to fail. Would you feel about giving a student an *F* on such an assignment? Probably not. This is one of the biggest problems with failure in the classroom: We set students up for "epic fails" before they have a chance to learn from the process. Instead, students need to be given multiple low-stakes opportunities to fail, as these facilitate ongoing risk taking and impart to students the sense that failure isn't as big as deal as they might think.

Though it may sound counterproductive, teachers should intentionally withhold some information from students during lessons to ensure that they experience failure. The idea that students need to have absorbed all of the expected content and skills before being asked to perform is a myth—in fact, approaching instruction in this way disconnects the experience of learning from the performance. Consider, for example, the common middle-school assignment

↳ isn't that what Connected Math is designed to do?

of writing a persuasive or argumentative paper. There are many criteria for assessing such assignments: proper spelling and grammar, a clear and compelling thesis, strong evidence and explanations, and so on. Asking that students become experts at each of these components before attempting to write a paper wouldn't make much sense.

Time

If we want students to experience failure as a means to success, then we must accord them the time necessary to experience it. One way to ensure that this happens is to design units that address multiple learning outcomes: For example, instead of just targeting a specific content standard on water quality in science class, teachers might also target a few literacy or scientific inquiry standards. Lesson units that address several standards at once give students the time to fail in one area while succeeding in others. The longer the lesson unit, the more time students have to try new ideas out, fail, and try again.

Game-Based Learning

By design, games of all sorts embrace failure as an essential component to eventual success. Wouldn't it be strange if you played an arcade game but weren't allowed to try multiple times to beat a level? Like game designers, educators need to consider the importance of "flow"—that is, the level at which difficulty and skill are aligned just enough for learning to occur (Csikszentmihalyi, 1990). When students are neither bored on the one hand nor anxious on the other, they are at their most receptive to learning from failures.

Game-based learning (GBL) has many applications in the classroom. One effective GBL strategy is to design lessons in the form of "quests" and "levels," so that students experience failure as an integral part of the learning journey. For example, one teacher I know transformed his French vocabulary lessons into a series of quests during which students were to guide a fictional French visitor around the school. Each quest focused on a different content objective: one on vocabulary, another verb conjugation, and so on. The quests varied in difficulty, and students were allowed to choose the ones that they want to embark upon. Students were given multiple chances to complete the quests in any order of their choosing. Upon completion of the quests, the students were asked to complete the "boss level," in which the various components of the unit were synthesized and "gamified" to encourage risk taking.

Many off-the-shelf games that weren't originally intended for use in the classroom can also have practical educational applications. Students can learn about narrative writing and even the concept of supply and demand by playing World of Warcraft, for example, or about math and physics by playing Minecraft. Of course, there are also many games designed with education specifically in mind that align to curriculum and content standards.

Project-Based Learning

Many elements of project-based learning (PBL) rely on failure as a mechanism for learning, including inquiry, critique and revision, and "voice and choice" (Larmer & Mergendoller, 2010). By choosing to use PBL in the classroom, teachers are committing to both leveraging and scaffolding failure in the instructional process. During the inquiry process, students research and try out new ideas, some of which they soon realize are mistaken. When students have a voice in and a choice of how they spend their time in the classroom, they are more likely to buy into lessons and feel comfortable taking risks.

Makerspaces

Many school and classrooms have Makerspaces in their classrooms where students can freely tinker with objects and try to create new things or experiment in the service of an assigned design challenge. The process of tinkering requires continual trial and error during which students will both fail and make breakthroughs. Makerspaces are safe, low-stakes, and accepting of all comers.

Computer Coding

Not only does computer coding support critical-thinking and problem-solving skills, it does so in an exceptionally safe environment where failure is almost inevitable. Many apps and websites allow students to code for free at a grade-appropriate level. One teacher I know has her first-grade students engage in an hour of coding every year by having them use simple directional programing to make a digital robot move from one level to another. Students are allowed as many attempts as necessary to make their coding work.

Questioning Strategies

As students fail in the classroom, they need to know how to uncover why they failed and what they can do to improve. We can help students to fail forward by taking the time to explicitly teach them questioning strategies by modeling everything from straightforward yes-or-no questions to deeper, more provocative ones. For example, let's say students are trying to research the causes of World War II but finding conflicting information. Rather than directly provide them with answers, the teacher might help students *develop the questions that they need to ask* to find those answers, perhaps by using stems along the following lines:

- "When did _____?"
- "What is _____?"
- "How is _____ related to _____?"
- "What evidence supports _____?"

Through the explicit teaching of questioning strategies, teachers can support students in moving past failure to success.

[handwritten margin note: Teacher poses more questions instead of giving answers]

Intentional But Flexible Grouping

Decisions about student grouping should be both intentional and flexible enough to allow input from students. If students fail to make the most effective grouping decision, chances are that they can learn from the failure. We have to be comfortable enough as teachers to let go and allow students to choose poorly when selecting a partner or team. When this does happen, teachers can intervene, provide students with other options, and ask them to reflect on what they might do differently next time. In this way, even unproductive collaborative learning can lead to productive learning.

What might you do differently next time?

Activities to Build Creative Skills

Building creativity can help students to embrace failure. By intentionally teaching and assessing different aspects of creativity, we can help not only to demystify creativity but also to give students specific creativity skills. Consider, for example, the Thinking Hat activity for building creative skills. In this activity, students wear different colored hats to represent different types of reactions to ideas (e.g., gray for naysaying, yellow for welcoming). This activity helps students to think outside the box by adopting different perspectives. Another good creativity-building activity is Alternative Uses, in which the teacher gives groups of students various items (e.g., a mug, a pencil) and asks them to come up with new uses for them.

Team-Building Activities

When we fail, we can learn from others how best to work through our failure. In fact, a shared understanding of norms about failure is critical. Teachers should engage students in collaborative team-building activities to meet shared goals. Teachers should select low-stakes activities and games for students in which they are encouraged to make mistakes and correct them together. These activities and games should focus on sharing and evaluating ideas and strategies, coming to consensus, and respecting one another. One example is the Human Knot strategy, where students try to undo a knot they've created together. Another strategy is to blindfold students and ask them to cross a room with safe obstacles in their way as their classmates coach and guide them. This strategy helps students to develop communication skills by coaching each through the failures.

Teachers should ask students to reflect on their collaborative skills and assess themselves and one another using rubrics and checklists that articulate what high-quality collaboration looks, feels, and sounds like. A culture of collaboration must be sustained year-round if the freedom to fail is to be ingrained.

Strategies for Modeling Risk Taking, Failure, and Celebration

Modeling is a powerful way to make transparent the thinking process behind a skill. Why not then use it to make transparent the process of failing toward success? Educators should model learning from failure as often as they can. For example, one teacher I know makes it a point to model failure when teaching long division to her elementary students. Instead of showing only the correct steps, she intentionally makes place-value errors and acknowledges them out loud to make her incorrect thinking visible ("I thought I did the steps correctly, but I seem to be getting the wrong answer according to the answer key. I guess I need to go back and walk through the steps again."). The teacher then asks her students for help arriving at the correct answer—and when she does, she celebrates her success with students. Once teachers have exposed their students to modeled failure, they can ask students to think aloud and admit their own failures (and the thinking processes behind them) as they work. In this way, failure is taken out of the shadows of the learning process.

Frequent Revision and Reflection

Educators need to create sacred spaces for students to continually reflect on what's working, what isn't, and why. Reflection focused on analyzing failure can help students to reframe it as a positive and meaningful experience. One teacher I know has her elementary students design digital stories about an animal of their choice. At various steps along the way, the teacher would check in to see how the students were doing. Although there weren't many failures in the early stages, everything changed when students were given the technology with which to create their final products. Although the teacher taught her students how to use the technology, many of them still struggled—specifically with pacing, timing, and lining up the images and animations they had produced. When the teacher noticed that her students had become visibly frustrated, she asked them to take a break and have students write a short reflection using words and pictures to show what happened, why they thought they had failed, and what they could do to make the digital story work. She also had the students select three goals or strategies that they would employ on their next attempt. The teacher knew it was time for students to use their metacognitive skills to assess their failures and fail forward. After collecting her students' reflections, she affirmed their failures through discussion and had them share out their strategies as a class. Students were less frustrated now that they knew they had more opportunities to try again. Consider using journals, discussions, and other reflection methods to facilitate failing forward.

Appropriate Scaffolding and Extension Work

During a unit, teachers will often check for understanding so that they can know how much their students are learning. These check-ins allow teachers to plan appropriate scaffolding for students. Scaffolding is about "saving" students—it's about giving them just enough help to be able to try, fail, and eventually succeed. It's important for teachers to consider how scaffolding can lead students to struggle productively.

We all have students who tend to finish tasks early or who have some background knowledge that makes work a bit easier for them. We need to make sure that these students experience failures, too. When you plan activities and instructional events, consider how you might challenge students by throwing a wrench into things. Give them more challenging criteria to meet or a more challenging way to show what they have learned

All of the strategies can be used not only as singular components of instruction, but also in tandem. Educators can start where they feel comfortable, using either strategies with which they're already familiar or building upon their "bag of tricks" to include more opportunities for intentional failure.

Failure and Assessment

Freedom to fail can be made or broken through assessment practices. If your assessment processes don't celebrate failure, then students will not embrace failure as a learning opportunity. Assessments that encourage the freedom to fail allow for student voice and choice and structured feedback. Here are some assessment principles and practices to bear in mind when encouraging productive failure in the classroom.

Pre-Assessment

When we pre-assess students, we are checking to see how they're progressing in their learning and ensuring that they have targeted learning outcomes that they know they must meet. Pre-assessment allows us to anticipate failures that students are likely to encounter and to consider whether we want to intervene or allow the failure to happen. If during my pre-assessment I notice that a specific student will probably experience numerous failures, I may scaffold that student's learning a bit so that he or she can feel at least some success; conversely, if I see that a student will probably not face much struggle, I may plan extension work for him or her.

Small Benchmarks for Failure

One of the most important things that teachers can do to reframe failure as productive is to ensure that instances of failure aren't too difficult to surmount by creating discrete assessment benchmarks within each task. For example, instead of bundling all of the assessed components of an essay into a single grade, teachers might break the assessment down into several grades: one for the thesis and introductory paragraph, one for the first few body paragraphs, one for the conclusion, and so forth. Smaller, targeted failures prevent students from becoming overwhelmed and allow them to see failure as integral to the journey rather than simply the result of it.

Formative Assessment

Formative assessment is critical to promoting the freedom to fail. In fact, failures serve as critical components of formative assessment: We must analyze student failures to understand the most effective next steps. By both looking at students' work and having discussions with students, we can identify gaps in learning and find ways to bridge them.

Consider Mary, a student who is designing an experiment to test the safety of the water in the school building. She will need to learn the processes of scientific inquiry to deduce the chemistry and quality of the water. Because the experiment will time to complete, Mary's teacher has planned specific benchmarks along the way both to hold students accountable and moving forward and to check for understanding.

When Mary hands in a draft science lab proposal, her teacher notices that the procedures aren't clearly worded and in fact would not serve to properly test her hypothesis. When she sits down with Mary to give her feedback, the teacher purposely doesn't tell her about some of the errors in the proposal so as to give her an opportunity to identify and correct them on her own. In this example, the lab proposal serves as a formative assessment. The same teacher also has her students reflect upon their learning in daily journals at the end of class, asking them general questions ("What are three important things you learned today?") and more specific questions about the content ("What did you learn about pH levels today?"). She collects the journals and reviews them to see evidence of learning and to uncover any misconceptions. Teachers need to use formative assessment to decide if they need to advance the lesson through whole group instruction, guided instruction, collaborative learning, or some other instructional model.

S.M.A.R.T Goals

S.M.A.R.T., in this case, stands for

- Specific,
- Measurable,
- Attainable,
- Reasonable, and
- Time-oriented.

S.M.A.R.T. goals allow students to have a voice in the assessment process by revisiting and reflecting openly on their learning. Failure can be daunting for students, and S.M.A.R.T. goals allow teachers to mitigate their anxiety while also scaffolding next steps. Goals that do not meet the S.M.A.R.T. criteria are less likely to move student forward through strategic failure.

Critique Protocols

Teachers can use critique protocols to ensure that constructive classroom feedback is focused, timely, and inoffensive. These can be modeled in a Fishbowl-style circle for the whole class before breaking into smaller groups for more efficient critiquing.

Mistakes vs. Errors

As teachers uncover student failures, they must distinguish between those due to mistakes and those due to errors. If a failure is due to a mistake, then the teacher can use prompts and cues to help students realize what they've done and make the corrections themselves. If, however, a failure is due to an error, then teachers need to address the errors directly. If an error isn't promptly and effectively addressed, then the student will have difficulty overcoming the attendant failure.

Redos

Allowing students to redo assignments, assessments, and other components of classwork can be a little bit tricky. Teachers must consider students' learning needs on the one hand and the reality of time constraints on the other when allowing students to redo assignments. If students aren't given the opportunity to correct their errors or mistakes, then they will not take risks and fail forward to succeed. Before offering students the chance to redo an assignment, teachers must help students fill in any learning gaps if their initial failure is to prove productive.

Effective Feedback

If students are going to fail forward, then they need to receive specific, relevant, and timely feedback. We want students to think and reflect on their failures and reach an understanding of what happened and what to do next, and we want them to apply the feedback to their work immediately. Teachers also need to ensure that feedback isn't too overwhelming, lest students not be able to internalize it and fail forward in a focused way.

Teachers should provide students with oral feedback organically while checking for understanding (e.g., "I noticed you chose to include a quotation in your paper. Where is the quote from? Who said it?" "The next step is a challenge. Make sure watch your decimal points!"). Written feedback should also be timely, particularly if it is related to an important benchmark that synthesizes several skills and content ideas. Written feedback should be aligned to specific, measurable goals that, ideally, are outlined in a rubric. Remember, too, that effective feedback need not only come from teachers: Peers and real-world experts are also good sources, especially if we ourselves are pressed for time.

Portfolios

The process of learning—failures included—can be effectively captured through the use of portfolios. When portfolios document failures alongside successes, students see the connection between the two. Portfolios can include rough drafts, reflections, and explanations of next steps. (In the case of digital portfolios, videos can be included as well.) Teachers can ensure that students' portfolios include both successes and failures by having them produce and include many drafts of their projects as well as written reflections on what worked and what didn't.

Grading

Students should not be graded on their failures, no matter how important they are to eventual success. If students fail and receive a poor grade, they will think that they're being punished for taking risks. Instead, teachers should use grades to reward students at their best. Failure should be motivated by authentic learning and risk taking rather than by grades.

I know a teacher who used to grade every assignment in his classroom and use the average for each student's final grade. Some of his students would begin a unit with fairly poor grades and gradually improve over time, which meant that their final grades were considerably lower than their scores on the final assessment. Reflecting upon this quandary, the teacher decided to make some changes to his grading policies: Though he continued to grade assignments throughout the unit, he allowed students to replace their final averaged grade with the grade they received on their summative assessment. He realized that he had previously been sending students mixed messages about risk taking and failure by essentially punishing them with a grade that didn't accurately reflect how much they had learned. Final grades should tell the story of failing forward, and students should be rewarded when they succeed. We need to let students know that we will honor their failures by rewarding them at their best. Assessment practices need to support the freedom to fail rather than work against it.

good idea

Failure as an Opportunity for Teacher Growth

A culture that supports the freedom to fail can only be successful if everyone is on the same page—students will not embrace failure if teachers don't as well. To this end, teachers need to get together and jointly reflect on the degree to which they are embracing failure in their work. In the classroom, teachers need to model the principles of failing forward every day. It is just as important for teachers to experience failure as it is for students.

Taking Transparent Risks

Taking transparent risks with students can be the best professional development strategy of all. Most teachers feel pressured to be infallible, which can have the unintended consequence of harming the school culture. When we admit something isn't working, we communicate the message that failure is simply an opportunity to reflect and revise. For example, if a lesson doesn't work out well, teachers can and should express the reasons why and even apologize. The same goes for trying out something new that they are not sure will work: "I'm trying something new today, and I am taking a risk. I really want to hear your feedback on it."

Educator Rita Pierson offers an instructive example of risk-taking transparency in a 2013 TED Talk video (Pierson, 2013). In it, she recounts the time she learned, following a lesson, that she had been teaching ratios incorrectly to her students. She apologized to her students, and they accepted her apology. In such cases, teachers can model perseverance by approaching their lessons in a new way and telling students that they are doing. Being transparent with risks will encourage students to take risks as well as build trust among them.

Observing Each Other's Failures and Successes

Professional development isn't simply a matter of attending workshops—it's also accomplished by observing other teachers in action. We need to be willing to open doors to colleagues and to visit their classrooms on occasion. If we observe each other more often and work to build a culture of trust, we can more readily identify failures. We've all been there, and when we are transparent about it, we can learn from the experience. Invite other teachers into your classroom when you plan to try something new; the feedback they give you get could be a game changer. Protocols and systems like instructional rounds can be used for support in these cases. Leaders need to create structures and system cycles that allow for more classroom observations, and observations should be considered sacred and never interrupted. Frequent, nonevaluative observations can alleviate the fear of failure and facilitate a growth mindset for teachers. Leaders need to facilitate a culture of collaboration and open doors: When the doors are open, both failures and successes become transparent to the school community.

PLCs and Collaboration

Professional learning communities (PLCs) and collaborative planning in general can help teachers create a culture of risk taking in their schools. It is important that collaboration be structured with a view toward failing forward, and PLCs are particularly effective in this regard as they tend to feature safety norms and thus are safe environments in which to take risks.

PLCs should be scheduled and held regularly—they shouldn't come out of the blue. When teachers know that they will receive feedback on an ongoing basis, they are more likely to share their work and take the risks associated with doing so; they are less afraid to share drafts or works in progress using protocols to create a structure for feedback and reflection.

Celebrating School Successes and Journeys

We don't celebrate nearly as much as we should for all the great work we do as teachers. It's important to seize opportunities to recognize both successes and productive failures as a way of modeling celebration for students. Teachers should share their stories of successes and failures with fellow teachers, whether in public ceremonies, peer-facilitated small groups, or more personal one-on-one moments.

One colleague of mine was really struggling to reach a particular student who seemed entirely unwilling to learn. After reaching out to his coworkers for support and new ideas, the teacher began to see a transformation in his student, who was starting to perform and produce work. To celebrate this breakthrough, the teacher shared his story with the rest of the school staff. It served as a moment of affirmation not only for the teacher, but for the school as a whole. It is crucial that we recognize celebrations regularly if we are to build a culture where failure is seen in a positive and non-punitive light.

Asking for Help

We all need to know how effective we are being as teachers. Principals, assistant principals, and other school leaders should frequently visit classrooms to provide teachers with low-stakes feedback. If you are struggling with a specific issue, reach out to these leaders as well as to your fellow teachers. Leverage technology and professional learning networks to support your growth: One teacher I know who was really struggling with formative assessments took to Twitter asking for help and received a raft of ideas from other teachers in the field. We will only be able to fail forward if we know that we've failed early on, and we need to take some responsibility and ask for support. By the same token, we should be willing to offer help to colleagues who reach out for help.

To give your feedback on this publication and
be entered into a drawing for a free ASCD
Arias e-book, please visit
www.ascd.org/ariasfeedback

ASCD | arias™

ENCORE

CHECKLIST FOR ENSURING THE FREEDOM TO FAIL

1. Teachers, students, and outside experts regularly frame failure as a positive concept.

2. It is common to celebrate both successes and productive failures on an ongoing basis.

3. Asking questions is valued and encouraged in the classroom.

4. There are high expectations for all students.

5. The setup of classrooms communicates that failure is an accepted norm.

6. Learning is authentic and mirrors "real-world" work.

7. Goals and expectations are clear and transparent to students.

8. Teachers require students to do rigorous and complex work.

9. Students showcase their learning through authentic products.

10. Teachers and school leaders provide sufficient time for the process of failing forward to yield results.

11. Teachers intentionally plan for student failures in their lesson designs.

12. Student failures are small rather than "epic."

13. Teachers use instructional strategies that support the freedom to fail.

14. Feedback to students is timely, meaningful, and effective.

15. Teachers assess the learning process as well as products of learning.

16. Students have ample opportunities for redos.

17. Students critique one another's work.

18. Grading structures take into account the importance of providing students with multiple opportunities to fail.

19. Assessments tell a story of the learning journey.

20. Formative assessments are frequent and ongoing.

21. Teachers use formative assessment to guide instruction based on both failures and successes.

22. Students reflect on their failures and successes.

23. Teachers intentionally scaffold creativity skills and growth mindsets.

24. Teachers are willing to admit mistakes and failures and model how to work through them.

Acknowledgments

I'd like to thank my parents, for allowing me to play video games throughout the years to foster my own learning through failure; my sister, for being a gamer right beside me; Doug Fisher and Nancy Frey, for their continued mentorship regarding instruction and assessment; and my fellow educators and consultants, for pushing me to write and share my ideas with others.

References

Csikszentmihalyi, M. (1990). *Flow: The psychology of optimal experience.* New York: Harper and Row.

Daggett, W. R. (2014). *The Rigor/Relevance Framework.* Rexford, NY: International Center for Leadership in Education.

Dweck, C. S. (2006). *Mindset: The new psychology of success.* New York: Ballantine.

Fisher, D., & Frey, N. (2014). *Better learning through structured teaching.* Alexandria, VA: ASCD.

Fisher, D., & Frey, N. (2012). *How to create a culture of achievement in your classroom.* Alexandria, VA: ASCD.

Fisher, D., & Frey, N. (2012, September). Making time for feedback. *Educational Leadership, 70*(1), 42–46.

Hoerr, T. R. (2013). *Fostering grit.* Alexandria, VA: ASCD.

Larmer, J., & Mergendoller, J. R. (2010). *Eight essentials for project-based learning.* San Francisco: The Buck Institute for Education.

Maxwell, J. C. (2007). *Failing forward: Turning mistakes into stepping stones for success.* Nashville, TN: Thomas Nelson.

McInnerney, J., & Robert, T. S. (2004). Collaborative or cooperative learning? In T. S. Roberts (Ed.), *Online collaborative learning: Theory and practice,* 203–14. Hershey, PA: Information Science Publishing.

Miller, A. (2014). How can project-based learning motivate students even further? *ASCD InService.* Available: http://inservice.ascd.org/how-can-project-based-learning-motivate-students-even-further/

Miller, A. (2013, March). Yes, you can teach and assess creativity. *Edutopia.* Available: http://www.edutopia.org/blog/you-can-teach-assess-creativity-andrew-miller

Pierson, R. F. (2013, May). Every child deserves a champion [presentation]. *TED Talks Education.* Available: https://www.ted.com/talks/rita_pierson_every_kid_needs_a_champion

Roschelle, J., & Teasley, S. (1995). The construction of shared knowledge in collaborative problem solving. In C. E. O'Malley (Ed.), *Computer supported collaborative learning,* 69–97. Heidelberg: Springer-Verlag.

Smith, K. A. (1995). *Cooperative learning: Effective teamwork for engineering classrooms.* Paper presented at the annual ASEE/IEEE Frontiers in

Education Conference, Atlanta. Available: http://fie-conference.org/
   fie95/2b5/2b54/2b54.htm

Tugend, A. (2011). The role of mistakes in the classroom.
   Edutopia. Available: http://www.edutopia.org/blog/
   benefits-mistakes-classroom-alina-tugend

U. S. Department of Education. (2013). *Promoting grit, tenacity, and perseverance: Critical factors for success in the 21st century.* Washington,
   DC: Author.

Van Der Veer, R. (2007). *Lev Vygotsky.* New York: Continuum International Publishing Group.

Wiggins, G., & McTighe, J. (2013) *Essential questions: Opening doors to
   student understanding.* Alexandria, VA: ASCD.

Willis, J. (2014, December 6). Personal communication.

Related Resources

At the time of publication, the following ASCD resources were available (ASCD stock numbers appear in parentheses). For up-to-date information about ASCD resources, go to www.ascd.org. You can search the complete archives of *Educational Leadership* at http://www.ascd.org/el.

Fostering Grit: How do I prepare my students for the real world? (ASCD Arias) by Thomas R. Hoerr (#SF113075)

Learning and Leading with Habits of Mind: 16 Essential Characteristics for Success by Arthur L. Costa and Bena Kallick (#108008)

The Motivated Student: Unlocking the Enthusiasm for Learning by Bob Sullo (#109028)

Inspiring the Best in Students by Jonathan Erwin (#110006)

Checking for Understanding: Formative Assessment Techniques for Your Classroom (2nd ed.) by Douglas Fisher and Nancy Frey (#115011)

How to Give Effective Feedback to Your Students by Susan M. Brookhart (#108019)

Total Participation Techniques: Making Every Student an Active Learner by Pérsida Himmele and William Himmele (#105001)

WHOLE CHILD The Whole Child Initiative helps schools and communities create learning environments that allow students to be healthy, safe, engaged, supported, and challenged. To learn more about other books and resources that relate to the whole child, visit www.wholechildeducation.org.

For more information: send e-mail to member@ascd.org; call 1-800-933-2723 or 703-578-9600, press 2; send a fax to 703-575-5400; or write to Information Services, ASCD, 1703 N. Beauregard St., Alexandria, VA 22311-1714 USA.

About the Author

Andrew K. Miller is an educational consultant specializing in formative assessment, project-based learning, and technology integration. He has taught English, social studies, and technology in both traditional and non-traditional secondary schools and is a frequent writer for ASCD and *Edutopia*. Readers can contact him via email at andrew@andrewkmiller.com.

WHAT KEEPS YOU UP AT NIGHT?

ASCD Arias begin with a burning question and then provide the answers you need today—in a convenient format you can read in one sitting and immediately put into practice. Available in both print and digital editions.

THE 5-MINUTE TEACHER

FOSTERING GRIT
Thomas R. HOERR

GRADING AND GROUP WORK
Susan M. BROOKHART

TEACHING WITH TABLETS
Nancy FREY Douglas FISHER Alex GONZALEZ

Answers You Need
from Voices You Trust

ASCD | arias™

For more information, go to www.ascdarias.org or call (toll-free in the United States and Canada) 800-933-ASCD (2723).

www.ascdarias.org